HOW TO PAINT & DRAW
LANDSCAPES

Written by
Alfred Daniels

CRESCENT BOOKS
New York

Acknowledgments

The Publishers would like to thank the following for permission to reproduce their photographs: Colour Library International 29, 42, 44, 46, 50, 56: The Trustees of the National Gallery 8, 9, 41, 59, 63, 64; The Tate Gallery, London 33, 62.

Illustrations provided by Tudor Humphries 15, 38, 39, 46, 47, 48, 49; Malcolm Henwood 17, 19, 21, 22, 23, 24, 25, 26, 27, 28, 30, 32, 41, 42, 44, 53, 58, 63; Martin Reiner 10, 11, 29, 34, 35; Gavin Rowe 6 (cover design for "Landslip" written by David Rees. Reproduced by kind permission of Hamish Hamilton Ltd.), 7, 20, 21; Andrew Skilleter 43; John Thompson 24, 25, 45, 57, 60, 61; Michael Vicary 40, 41, 54; Paul Wright 23, 26, 27, 31, 36, 37, 50, 51, 52, 53.
Additional artwork by Liz Chapman; Tony Streek.

Designed and produced by Intercontinental Book Productions Limited, Berkshire House, Queen Street, Maidenhead, Berkshire SL6 1NF.

Contents

Introduction

Landscape is probably the most popular of all the subjects that a painter has to choose from, possibly because it is the most accessible. Any landscape is acceptable as a starting point for a good painting. Conversely, a beautiful scene can produce disappointing results if one or two fundamental technical and aesthetic points have not been grasped.

This book has been designed to lead you through the problems you may encounter, and help you tackle them in a practical and creative way, so that you may enjoy and express yourself even if you are a beginner.

You will be introduced to drawing and painting materials and their various methods of employment. Problems of composition, structure, light and shade, and color mixing are dealt with as simply as possible. Techniques for painting trees, clouds, skies, water, and different kinds of terrain are explained fully and simply with step-by-step illustrations and a variety of useful hints to help you.

The book also gives an insight into how the great landscape painters approached and solved the problems involved, and how you can benefit by a study of their methods.

How To Paint and Draw Landscapes provides the beginner with a complete basic course about materials and methods.

Subject and media

The wide variety of materials and the range of subject matter available means that you will need to master a certain number of basic skills in order to be able to paint successfully. Learning to diversify the way you use your materials is a necessary part of the process of painting.

Landscape painting is concerned with nature, and nature can be perverse. The bright day can turn dull, sunshine turn to rain, heat to cold, and vice versa. The time of year, weather, and light will also affect the way you go about your work and your approach may need to be modified. For example, you may find mixing your drawing with watercolor washes more suitable than using them separately when an unexpected situation arises. Conversely, your original intention to draw in pencil alone may need to be expanded by the addition of pen and ink.

Above: *A detail of a painting executed for a book cover. It was produced using a variety of media and a number of the techniques discussed in this book.*

Right: *A study broadly handled in oil paint. The color is important: note how the red of the building lifts and intensifies the greenish yellow of the foreground.*

Flexibility is not only necessary to cope with the unexpected, but frequently produces much more exciting results. Moreover, being flexible in the way you work means that you will often surprise yourself with what you do and so be less afraid of taking chances or experimenting.

The freer, more spontaneous mixed media studies, however far short of your intentions they may fall, can always be "worked up" later in your studio. Though many landscape artists prefer to complete work on the spot, it is not always possible, and mixed-media or spontaneous studies will often excite you enough to continue them later. In short, you must learn not to be put off by the unexpected, or risk producing fragmentary and dull work.

Nature is full of surprises; the ability to use a variety of materials and techniques will enable you to capture the diversity that nature displays. The only way to obtain this ability is by constant practice with different materials and techniques.

Above: *Watercolor was used over a pencil drawing to describe the crisp and subtle color of a landscape under snow.*

Left: *The heat of the desert under a baking sun has a flattening effect. The opacity and flatness of gouache is the ideal medium to portray this.*

Historical development

The landscape has been used as a motif throughout the history of art. In the West, however, its importance was relegated, initially, to providing merely a background to a thematic subject or a setting for a portrait. Often the landscape was used as decoration or as a symbol. Rarely in the great periods of art was it represented as a subject in its own right.

By the seventeenth century it began to acquire greater importance, and figures, themes, and landscapes became a more unified whole. This can be clearly seen in the work of Giorgione and Titian and, later, in the paintings of Rubens, Patenier, and Breughel, the landscape becomes the dominant feature.

These paintings, as with the "Classical" landscapes of Claude and Poussin, were still mainly produced in the studio from studies or from memory, or were invented. Painters like Gainsborough built little models of earth, moss, rocks, and plants in their studios and painted from them in the firm belief that they were painting landscapes.

The most significant change came at the end of the eighteenth century. For various reasons, disillusionment with accepted practice gave rise to the belief that nature had something more to offer. From the sketches of Constable to the poems of Wordsworth and the writings of John Ruskin, the worship of nature began to excite the imagination of the intelligentsia of the times.

For the painter, the study of nature changed his whole way of thinking and working. It brought him out of the studio and into the open air. He had to study and paint nature "on the spot", and was forced into a direct confrontation with nature instead of comfortably contriving landscapes in the studio. The whole course of landscape painting began to change; colors became more lively and intense, compositions more natural and less contrived. The devices used to contain and convey the composition were the natural lines of horizon and trees.

New techniques

The movement of clouds, water, weather, and seasons demanded a completely new approach, and to capture these changes meant that new techniques and methods had to be adopted. Painters had to work faster to do

Right: The Battle of San Romano *by Paolo Uccello illustrates the early use of landscape as a device to contain and intensify the statuesque quality of the figures and horses in the foreground.*

Right: *In Nicolas Poussin's* Landscape with a Man Killed by a Snake *the landscape is convincingly realistic. For all its classical beauty and attention to detail, however, it remains a support for the tragedy taking place in the foreground.*

justice to what they saw, giving rise to freer handling of oil paint. This can be seen in the paintings of Constable, Turner, and the Impressionists. This in turn gave painting more vitality and, most important, more spontaneity.

Another important development was in the use of watercolor. The beauty of watercolor was that artists could work with great speed. It is an ideal medium for working outside; it dries quickly, and can produce beautiful, convincing effects with the minimum of equipment. The artist's colormen also aided the advance by manufacturing more permanent and varied colors, which previously had been rather limited in range.

The modern approach

Today, when we think of landscape, we think of nature first. Landscape painting is not something made up or experienced at second hand. It is rooted in observation and response to nature. Most people look upon nature with affection, recognizing a special kind of beauty unaffected by man, and for many artists it is still a powerful source of inspiration and delight.

The newcomer to painting must look at and learn from the work of the artists of the past, their paintings can and will affect the way you work. Too many people approach landscape painting with the view that it is about scenes almost untouched by the hand of man. This is because the work of the artists of the nineteenth century, when landscape painting came of age, appears rural to the modern eye. However, the world was as modern to these artists as it is to us today. They studied it and produced statements of beauty and truth. Learn from them as opposed to copying them, and beware of nostalgia.

Right: *Corot was one of the first painters to work in the open air. His subject matter is also different; gone are the god-like figures in romantic settings.* Peasants Under the Trees at Dawn *shows ordinary people in an every day rustic setting.*

Right: *The English artist John Constable used many color sketches painted at speed from which he later produced large, highly finished canvases in the studio. This study of* Weymouth Bay *is painted over a warm ground which shows through the blue sky and gray of the sea. The beach and cliffs in the foreground consist totally of the ground color highlighted with detail.*

The purpose of drawing

The main aim of drawing should be to explore the elements and relationships of the world around us. The understanding of form that results from our efforts to analyze and respond to these things helps to develop awareness and the imaginative sense.

The process of learning to see objectively and analytically is a continual one which allows the gradual build-up of a store of knowledge. The search for visual truth will gradually add to your artistic vocabulary and this in turn will increase your ability to describe the physical world.

In every field of endeavor an understanding of the tools used and the objectives to be strived for is essential to progress and art is no exception. Both the conscious and the subconscious must be trained to perceive the components contributing to shape and form, and drawing is an essential tool for studying those situations you wish to explore. In the same way that a composer must understand the principles of sound and the characteristics and limitations of musical instruments in order to exploit them effectively, the artist must know his materials and be able to manipulate the qualities of shape, volume, texture, tone, and color.

Drawing and painting is always a self-educating process; you should learn something from everything you undertake. Each time you set pencil or brush to paper you should feel a sense of adventure more important than the finished result.

Drawings are necessary as a form of visual note-taking in preparation for further work and will concentrate on the basic elements of tone, form, and construction. They are also used to explain nature and function as in designer's drawings and can encapsulate information more efficiently than photographs.

Left: *It is in the initial sketch that the artist first defines the area in which he is interested. It is also useful as a means by which to check the composition and layout of the subsequent painting.*

Right: *More detailed studies abstracted from the scene should follow the initial sketch. Nothing is more frustrating than working from drawings that lack sufficient detail.*

Green on this tree
brighter than those in background

Blue tint to
chimney in shadow

Cool blue

Purple/Brown
Little rust

Red brickwork

Ground here white
in contrast with
shadows
to left of building

Bark on logs silver gray.
Wood, white where bark
has been stripped away

Umber shadows in foreground
turning to blue in middle distance

Rust color recurring
on wood and roofing

Above: *A simplified drawing of the scene with written notes is invaluable for remembering local colors and the general atmosphere of the surroundings.*

Left: *Another detail, this time in full color to supplement the color notes and the pencil sketches.*

Materials: oil color

Oil color is one of the most versatile of paints, which is why it has been used so widely and for so long. Apart from its historical pedigree, it is capable of great subtlety and vigor.

There is a vast range of colors, which mix well and are very pleasant to handle, to choose from. They can be used in a number of different ways: transparently in glazes, to show the underpainting, or opaquely to obliterate previous workings, allowing you to overpaint should the need arise. You can also paint thinly to create a smooth finish, or thickly to create tactile effects (Impasto). Application of the paint can be made with either hard bristle brushes or soft ones (sable hair or nylon) and palette or painting knives can also be used.

Oil colors are easily diluted with turpentine or linseed oil to make them flow better or they may be used straight from the tube to make an expressive brush mark. They can be blended smoothly together, or one color can be dragged over another (known as scumbling).

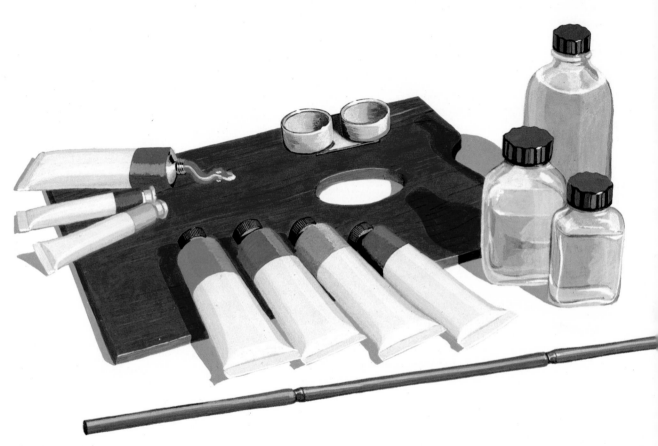

Brushes

Brushes come in all shapes and sizes, either of bristle or hair. Hog bristles are the most suitable for oil because they are stiffer and they mix and apply the paint rather better. Hair brushes, like sable, are better suited to watercolor work, but can be used with oils for fine detail. The four basic shapes are Round, Flat, Bright or Square, and Filbert. You need to choose three or four of medium size

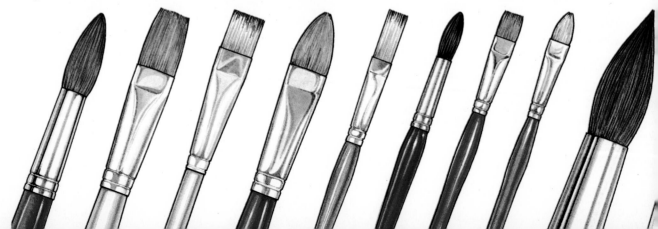

Easels

Like brushes, easels come in all shapes and sizes. They range from large studio types to the light sketching kind. Each manufacturer has a different way in which the angle of the easel may be adjusted. Some have seats and painting boxes combined. This can be an expensive item, so when choosing one bear the following points in mind.

Can you use it both indoors and out? Is it easily transportable? Will it do for both watercolors and oil? Whether made of metal or wood, strength is vital as is ease of handling; nothing is more annoying than an easel which collapses when you are halfway through a painting. Having a stool attached to an easel has its advantages but some painters prefer to stand. To avoid complications have a portable standing easel and take a lightweight stool with you so that you can adapt to the variation of local conditions.

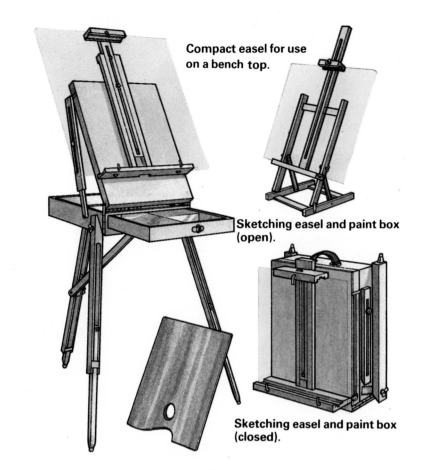

Compact easel for use on a bench top.

Sketching easel and paint box (open).

Sketching easel and paint box (closed).

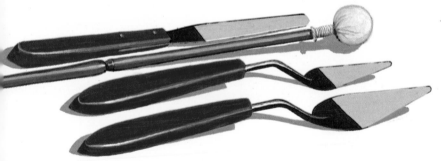

from these and add to them later. Get the best quality brushes as they wear better. Do not attempt to use a brush that is worn or splayed as you will not be able to control your brushwork properly. The condition of the brushes is important; they govern how you mix and apply the paint, so keep them clean.

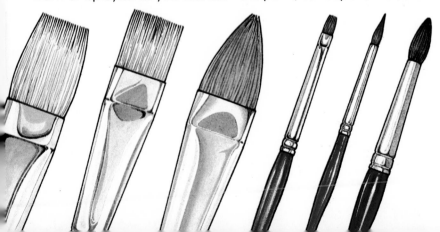

Palettes

A good palette is essential. It should be light in weight, not too small or too large and, for landscape painting, rectangular in shape for easy packing. A white plastic palette is ideal for a beginner because its color will allow him to judge his mixtures better. Many palettes are made of wood, and some are covered with plastic. In choosing one, bear in mind that it should be easy to hold and easy to keep clean. All the mixing is done on the palette so, when laying out your colors, leave plenty of room in the center. Arrange your colors systematically from light to dark. Attach your palette cup to the rim, away from the colors so that it does not spill into them. Keep your palette as clean as possible while you are painting, and when you have finished scrape the paint off the palette with a knife. If a wooden palette is used, this should be wiped over with linseed oil.

13

Surfaces

The most popular surfaces for oil painting are canvas, prepared boards or prepared paper. Canvas, probably the most pleasant to work on, can be obtained in a smooth or rough finish and is usually stretched on a wooden frame, called a stretcher, in various sizes up to 3½ feet wide. Though the most traditional surface, it has two disadvantages: it is both expensive and vulnerable to damage and decay. Prepared boards, on the other hand, are inexpensive and easily transported. They also come in grades from smooth to rough and are as good as canvas in many ways. Finally there is prepared paper, which is available in sheet form or in blocks, making it ideal for outdoor work. To begin with, try either the boards or paper and, when confident, progress to canvas.

Choosing colors

Mixing colors for the first time can be made more difficult by having too great a range on your palette. Manufacturer's catalogs list over a hundred but, for landscape painting, only a few colors are essential, and when you have mastered them, you can then add a personal selection. It is essential to learn to mix the colors you require. Do not imagine they can all be squeezed straight from the tube just when you need them. A good basic selection of colors will include: Cadmium Yellow, Cadmium Red, Alizarin Crimson, Viridian, Ultramarine, Monastral Blue, Raw Sienna, Raw Umber and Titanium White.

Linseed oil and turpentine are kept in the double palette cup. One cup can contain linseed oil and the other turpentine so that you can mix one with the other before adding to your paints. Oil alone can cause the painting to become slippery as work progresses because it dries far more slowly. This can lead to muddy colors.

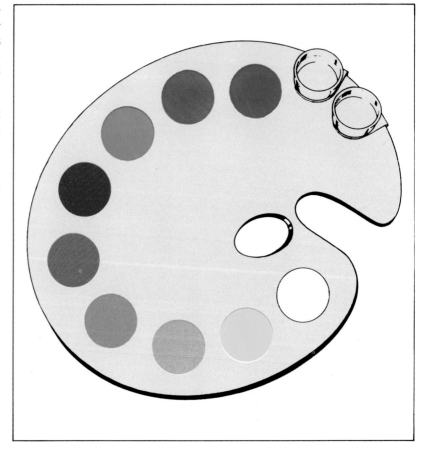

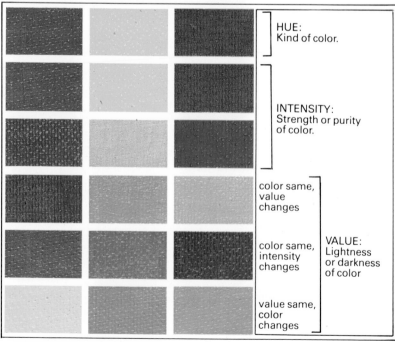

HUE:
Kind of color.

INTENSITY:
Strength or purity
of color.

color same,
value
changes

color same,
intensity
changes

VALUE:
Lightness
or darkness
of color

value same,
color
changes

Above: *The chart shows the three primary colors and, between these, the three secondaries giving some indication of the range that is available using red, yellow, and blue plus white.*

Left: *This chart will help you to understand some of the terms used when dealing with color.*

Materials: watercolor

Watercolor, as its name suggests, is water-soluble paint. Though technically less complicated to use than oils and requiring less equipment, the materials should be of the best quality and the selection should be considered carefully to achieve the best results that the subtle character of watercolor allows.

Paints

To produce watercolor paints, pigments are ground in gums with the addition of wetting agents and preservatives for ease of dilution and smoothness of flow. The colors are bought in tubes or pans; tubes are best for large paintings and pans for outdoor work as they are more easily carried in lightweight japanned boxes. The boxes are made of metal, and serve as a palette for mixing washes. Watercolor is a transparent medium that achieves its effect by the overlaying of washes of color. It is economical in use so purchase the best quality, which will reward you with sparkling results and delicate color. You will need about twelve half-pans to begin with; a selection will be suggested in the section on how to use watercolors.

Brushes

The best brushes for watercolor are made of sable hair; they can hold a good deal of water and the washes can be flooded on with greater control. A good brush will have a fine point which is used for detail work. They range from small, size 000, to large, size 14. The best will be expensive but they are a joy to use and produce the most beautiful results. With care they will last a lifetime. Begin with about three: sizes 4, 6, and 8. You can add others later.

Brushes are also made from ox or squirrel hair, or nylon. If you cannot afford sable, squirrel is the next best. Nylon brushes tend not to hold liquid as well as other types.

Easels and water

Easels are less necessary for watercolor work as you can rest your board on your knees. For comfort and for holding your board at the required angle, a portable seat is essential.

Clean water is vital to the production of clear colors, so choose a pot that is large enough to hold enough for both diluting the color in the palette and keeping the brushes clean.

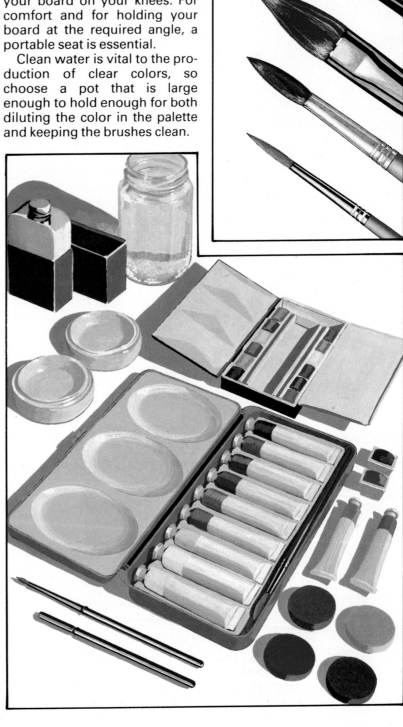

Watercolor paper

Paper for watercolor should be of the best quality. Water will wrinkle paper and ruin the appearance of a watercolor so the paper must be stretched. Papers come in many sizes and surfaces from smooth to rough, and you should try them all in time. For convenience you can also get blocks, pads, and cardboard — known as fashion boards, which are of a suitable size and ideal for outdoor work as they provide their own support for the work.

Stretching paper

You will need a drawing board, a roll of gummed brown paper strip, and a clean sponge. The paper can either be held under running water, or the water can be applied with a sponge while the paper is rested on a flat work surface.

Lay the paper on the drawing board, apply gummed paper strip round all edges so that half the strip is on the paper and half on the board. It should then be put aside while the paper dries slowly and naturally. The process can be repeated several times so that a number of layers are taped to the same area, creating a sketching block.

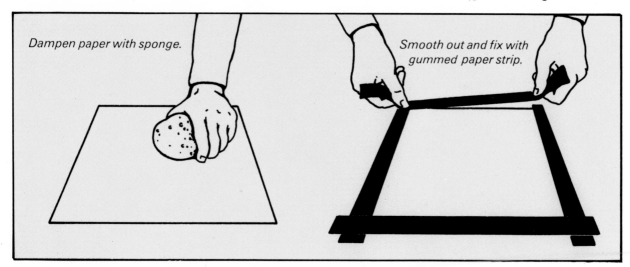

Dampen paper with sponge.

Smooth out and fix with gummed paper strip.

Materials: drawing

When working outdoors, speed is essential. Drawing provides for this admirably as the materials are easily carried and simple to use if you observe this simple dictum: a drawing is a tonal image that progresses from white to black; use as wide a range of tones as possible.

Pencils

The most common are produced from graphite ranging from 6H, which are very hard and give a gray mark, to 6B which are very soft and produce a blacker line. 2B is a good grade to begin with. Alternatively carbon pencils produce fine grays and rich velvety blacks which are less shiny than graphite pencil marks and less likely to lose their sparkle. Conté pencils in black and red are ideal for sketching, rather like carbon but softer and less easy to keep sharp. They can produce attractive results when red and black are used in combination. Charcoal pencils and wax crayons make interesting alternatives. Probably the most versatile of all are colored pencils. Some manufacturers provide a range which can be activated with water to produce washes of color and these are a useful

substitute for watercolor paints. Other media include felt-tip, fountain, and ball-point pens. Colored inks are useful as they can be used with pen or brush and in conjunction with carbon or lead pencil give attractive results.

You will also require a good quality eraser, preferably of the kneadable type so that you can shape it to a point. For the more powdery media such as conté and charcoal, you will need a can of fixative spray to prevent the work becoming smudged.

Right: *Each drawing material can be used in different ways to create a variety of effects.*

Below: *A range of ancillary drawing equipment.*

Bottom: *A range of drawing materials and typical marks.*
1: H pencil, 2: HB pencil,
3: 2B pencil, 4: 6B pencil,
5: HB carbon, 6: 3B carbon,
7: HB mechanical, 8: chinagraph,
9: charcoal hard and medium,
10: Derwent pencil, 11: Caran d'Ache watersoluble, 12: Caran d'Ache felt tip, 13: Derwent color block, 14: Talon pastel, 15: paper stump.

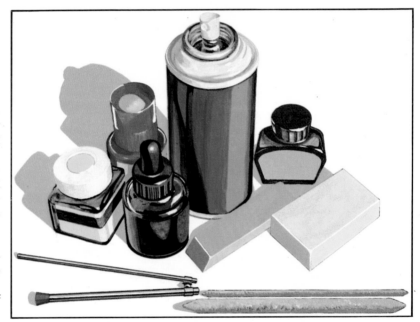

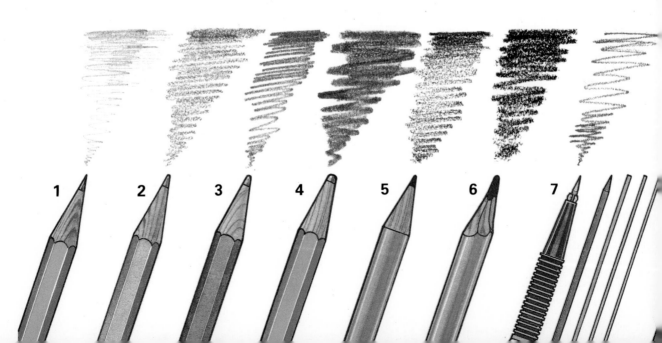

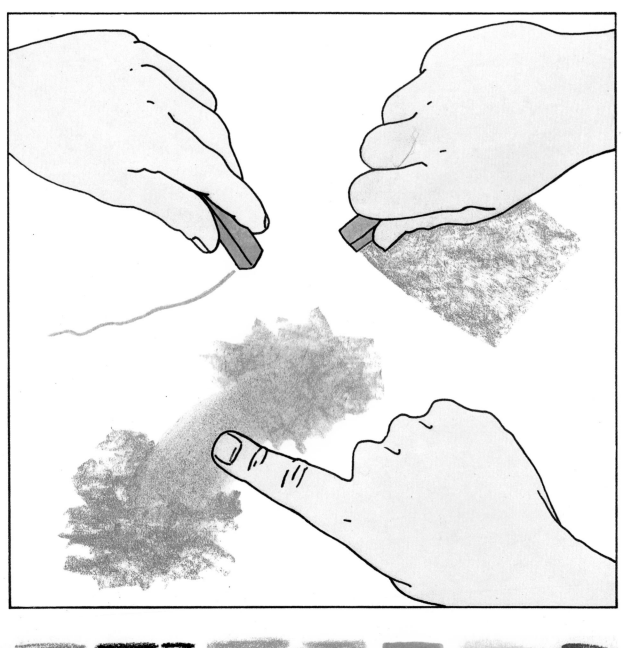

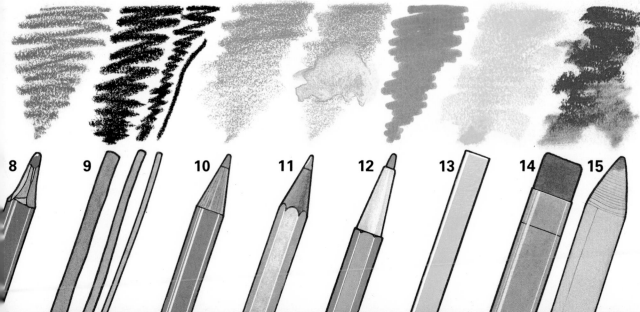

Sketching

A sketch is a preliminary, and often unfinished, drawing or painting. Used experimentally, it can help you learn about technique, or as a means of self-expression. As a rough draft for a finished work without detail but with broad outlines, a sketch can suggest ideas or be an enjoyable way of recording observations. It should be approached with confidence as an immediate and spontaneous way of expressing yourself. Sketches are often enjoyed for their own sake and are preferred by many to more finished work.

Sketching allows freedom to combine pencils with watercolor or pen and ink or both. You can begin with one and work over with the other. Or you can do two or more drawings of the same subject in different painting and drawing media.

Sketching should attempt to explore the possibilities of a scene, and differs from formal studies in that it will suggest rather than explain what is observed.

A sketch is, therefore, inclined to be a hit-or-miss affair, but therein lies its charm and also its usefulness to the beginner as a method of working. It may be more expendable, but often displays qualities that more finished works lack.

Sketching outdoors plays an important role in understanding landscape and a knowledge of the materials helps to produce good results. Simplicity is the keynote; be prepared for the un-

expected by taking a selection of materials, even if you have planned your excursion beforehand.

Sketchbooks

Hard-cover sketchbooks are a necessary part of your equipment. They keep your work together, the hard covers provide protection and act as a drawing board. They come in many sizes and many surfaces (11¾in. x 8¼in. is the most suitable). Some sketchbooks have a variety of different surfaced papers to allow for many ways of working. Fill your sketchbook consecutively. Do not jump about. Date and annotate sketches with written notes.

Satchels

Sketching materials should be light and portable. It is not always possible to use transport to the best spots and you may have to walk, so have a strong, light satchel to take pencils, pens, watercolors, brushes, and paper safely and comfortably.

Above: *The mood created by this sketch is one of calm repose.*

Opposite top: *The angular lines of the building in the background are contrasted with the natural shape of the trees.*

Opposite bottom: *In this sketch, the mountainous clouds are echoed and amplified by the rolling hills of the terrain beneath.*

Right: *A simple canvas roll can be made easily and cheaply and is invaluable for keeping your materials together.*

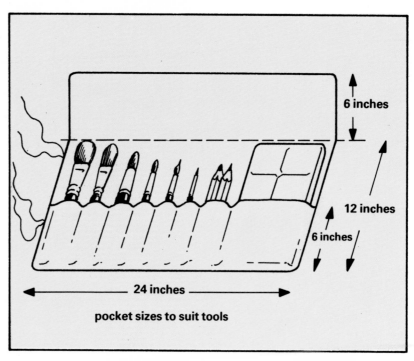

6 inches

12 inches

6 inches

24 inches

pocket sizes to suit tools

Composition: proportion and balance

Nature does not exist in a rectangle, whereas paintings do. Surfaces are generally rectangular and this means that we need to select and arrange what we see in order to ensure that our paintings are coherent and convincing. For this purpose we need to know something about composition.

There are two basic principles which are involved in the creation of a successful composition: proportion and balance, and rhythm and movement.

Proportion

Surfaces are available in landscape, portrait, or square format. Each shape has a characteristic thrust. In a horizontal rectangle the eye is encouraged to move across, in a vertical it moves up and down. In a square the thrusts are equal, creating a static composition, which is possibly why this format is not often used.

Landscapes, naturally, tend to fit better into horizontal rectangles. Nature, while it is full of variety and vitality, is always in harmony. The proportions are never seen to be equal. A rectangle, on the other hand, can be divided equally or unequally. Equal divisions tend to be static and lack vitality and

unequal ones tend to suggest movement. The "happiest" division which seems to enhance yet harmonize within a rectangle is a division of the rectangle into three parts. They may be equal thirds or unequal, upright or horizontal.

The difficulty with a symmetrical composition is that, though it may work with some kind of subject matter: still life, flower painting, portraits, and townscapes, it rarely works with landscape because it is not dynamic enough. Even the most carefully planned park cannot be symmetrically arranged on the support without looking unreal and therefore unconvincing.

Placing important objects like trees, buildings, farm equipment, gates, immediately in the center of the painting destroys the visual excitement and is likely to produce boredom.

Proportion is mainly concerned with the way in which you

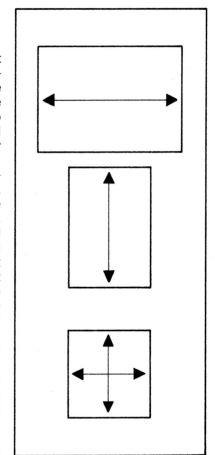

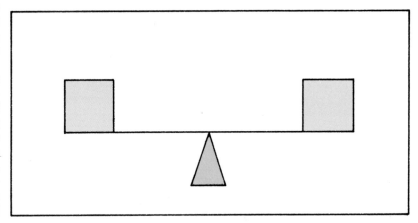

distribute the main areas of your composition.

The distribution of shapes and masses is the function of balance.

Balance

Balance in a composition is concerned with creating a center of interest or focal point that will not disrupt the unity of the whole, or be overwhelmed by other elements.

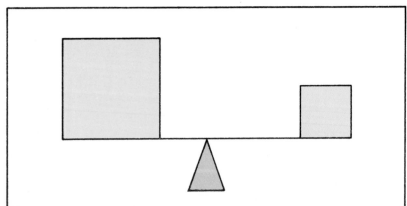

The eye continually moves from one point of interest to another in order to build a complete image in the mind. If points of interest are not properly related they will create an imbalance in the composition which will reduce and make trivial in the painting what was seen as dynamic in the original landscape. This is why most people at some time have taken a photograph of a breathtaking landscape only to be disappointed by the print obtained. The camera does not in itself emphasize a point of interest.

If the relationship of the parts of the composition are of equal visual weight and are symmetrically placed, the result will tend to look static and uninteresting. If, on the other hand, the parts are unequal and are asymmetrically placed, the result will be full of interest, movement, and contrast. It will be seen that asymmetrical compositions will be more suitable for landscape painting than symmetrical ones.

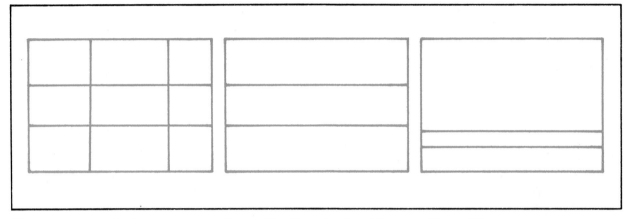

Opposite above: *The format of the paper suggests the visual thrust.*

Opposite below: *In these illustrations, both scales are in equilibrium but the lower one is more dynamic.*

Above: *The "happiest" division of any rectangle is into thirds. The proportions created by the division can vary considerably and the focal point can sit on a line or be encapsulated by them.*

Below: *The format of this painting is based upon the division shown in the illustration above. The focal point of the painting is the fields framed by the trees in the middle distance.*

Composition: rhythm and movement

The composition of any drawing or painting relies on a visual harmony created by the tension of the lines, masses, or color areas which exert a pull opposed by an equal pull in the opposite direction. The quality of any line, for example, will produce a direction and feel of its own: a smooth, curving line will lead the eye gently along its length and create a soothing effect, while a deeply incised erratic line will evoke tension and drama. It must be remembered that every directional pull has to be balanced, otherwise the observer's eye will be projected off the picture surface. Equilibrium is the essence of composition, but it should be an interesting equilibrium.

Visual movement

It is the rhythm and movement set up in a painting which should cause the eye to roam around the picture and arrive finally and inexorably at the focal point. From here it may well begin the journey again, possibly in a different way, but it should always return. If the eye is allowed to drift across the surface and finds nothing to interest it, there is something wrong with the composition.

The more the observer's eye is allowed to rove about the painting, the more interested it will be and the more it will be prompted

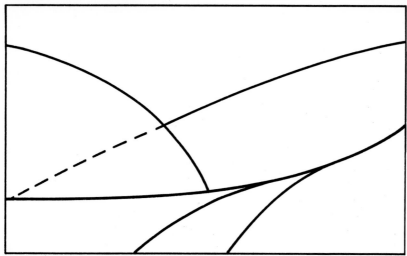

Above and left: *The direction lines of the keyline diagram show the main lines that the eye will follow or be affected by as it scans the painting.*

Opposite right: *The line formed by the pebbles and boulders on the bank leads the eye into the picture.*

Opposite far right: *In this painting the eye tends to rest upon the line of the hill in the foreground and scan across it looking at the view in the distance.*

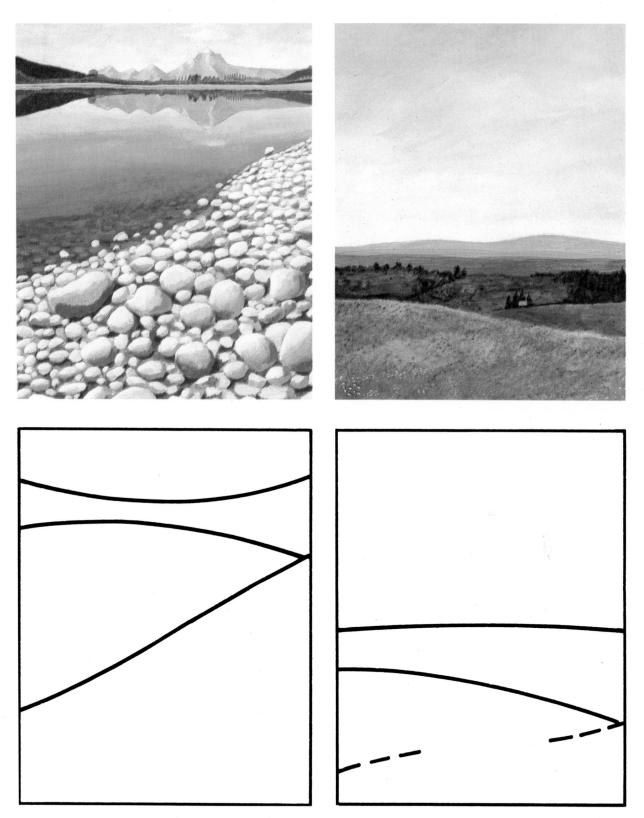

to look. To create controlled movement is not a difficult task if you consider the lines that you use and their direction; the eye will tend always to follow the length of a line – two lines in the same direction or a thick line will reinforce this tendency. The eye should, however, arrive at points which create the feeling that something similar has been seen before in the picture; this can be a device as simple as a repeated curve but it will set up a rhythm which produces unity in the whole. Good composition is a result of careful orchestration of shape, color and line.

Space in landscape: planes

We are able to move in a landscape because it is three-dimensional; but a painted surface is flat, having only two dimensions; height and width. The problems that this raises for the painter can be resolved by use of traditional pictorial devices: linear perspective, color perspective, and the conventions which may be derived from them.

The superimposition of various planes is one effective way of creating an illusion of depth. If you divide the distance from your position to the horizon line into three parts, you will have three separate areas to deal with.

The foreground is that plane nearest to you, the second is the middleground, and the third the background. Establish these planes immediately you begin, so that as you progress you can take each one to a different degree of finish. The background can be left lightly painted with a little more detail in the middleground. The foreground is painted with the greatest detail, thickest paint, and brightest colors, to pull it forward while the other two planes are pushed back.

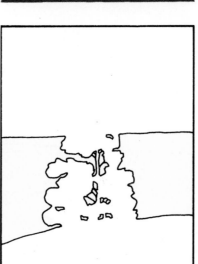

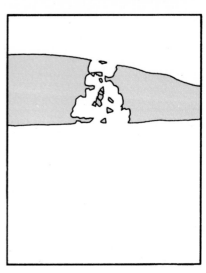

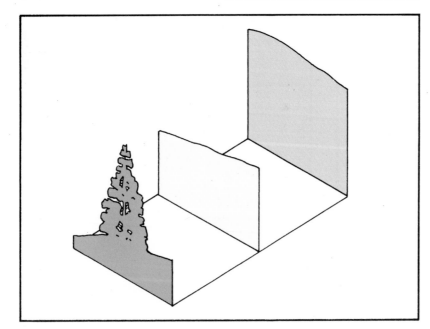

Above: *The illusion of depth can be created by treating the various areas of a scene as planes. Tonal value is the most important consideration in this kind of work.*

Left: *The planar structure of a painting suggests space in much the same way as stage scenery.*

Opposite: *The areas of the painting at the top of the page are illustrated by the keyline diagram underneath. Notice how each plane is suggested by a difference in both strength of color and the hardness of its edge.*

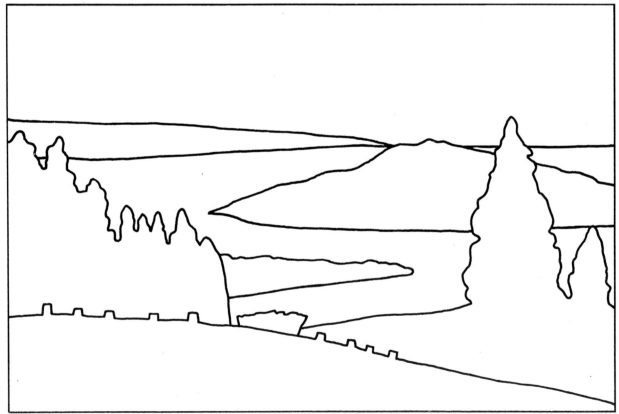

Space in landscape: linear perspective

A vast knowledge of perspective is not absolutely necessary for a landscape painter; he can achieve spatial depth convincingly by other means. There might be occasions when perspective is needed, however, and a grasp of the basic principles will be useful.

Linear perspective is a convention which was devised by architects of the fifteenth century to show their clients how their buildings would look before they were built. It should be realized that, like constructing planes on the canvas to create an illusion of depth, perspective is a convention, a tool which can be used to aid drawing from observation. There is, however, no substitute for clear observation, whatever you are drawing or painting.

The first thing to decide when doing a perspective drawing is the position of the eye level or

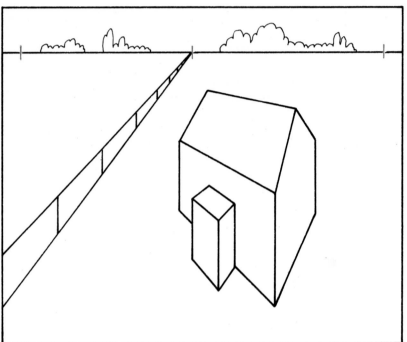

Left: *In this diagram, the eye level of the observer is high above the ground as if looking down upon the scene from the side of a hill. The fence which enters the field of vision at the lower left, meets the vanishing point on the horizon. In order to construct the house, two vanishing points are used. The basic rule of perspective is that all parallel lines meet at the same vanishing point which is always on the horizon.*

Right: *The scene viewed from a lower eye level. The same rules still apply. The vanishing points remain in the same position on the horizon line though some of the lines of the house are now angled downward because they are above eye level.*

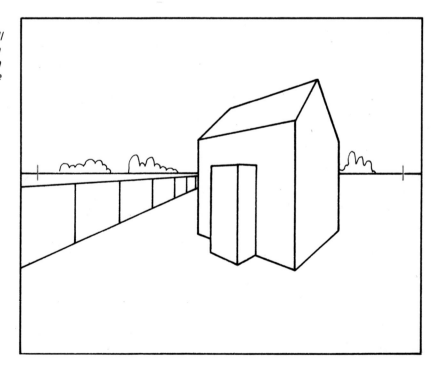

horizon line on the paper. This will depend on your position. Is it high or low?

If your eye level is high, so will be your horizon line on the paper and everything below it will slope up toward it.

If low, everything above the horizon line will slope downward to it.

If your eye level is midway, both upward and downward angles will appear equally distributed.

These angles which slope downward and upward are the core of perspective and can be seen clearly in places where the angles are most acute, such as in towns and villlages. In the open landscape, however, they are not so strongly in evidence. Use whatever clues you may find: buildings, roads, or fences.

You will observe that regular features, like a line of poles or a fence that recedes from you or even a road, will possess angles that you can assess. These angles which will slope upward toward your eye level, or downward if they are above your eye level, can be measured by holding a pencil vertically so that the angle can be assessed in relation to it.

Below: *As this drawing shows, the vanishing points will not always be contained within the confines of the picture area. The same rules of construction apply, however, and if necessary a larger sheet of backing paper could be used to check the position of the vanishing points as the work proceeds.*

Space in landscape: tonal perspective

It might not be immediately apparent, but tone plays as important a role in landscape painting as color. A painting, to be effective, is dependent on both.

What, then, is meant by tone? Tone is the degree of lightness or darkness of a color. As in music, if the tones are properly related the result will appear more harmonious and so be more expressive. If the tones are misjudged the result will be confused, and unattractive.

Normally, if the light is poor we cannot see color and cannot perceive distance as efficiently. This is why, when driving a car at dusk, we find it more difficult to judge speed and distance properly. There is not sufficient light to operate those cells in our eyes which perceive color, yet the cells still try and tend to confuse the message which reaches the brain from the cells which perceive only black and white. From a practical point of view, the eyes respond to tone more readily than they do to color; color is secondary.

A study of the tones of a landscape will enable you to use color to express distance far better. If tones are graded into their proper relationship, in our drawings and paintings, the eye will accept the illusion of distance.

Grading tone is not difficult. The darkest tones are closest while the lightest appear further away. The things closest to us are stronger in tone and color, are clearer in detail and, as they move from us in the distance they become blurred. If you make a point of emphasizing this in your paintings, you will have no difficulty in creating the illusion of great depth. Tonal color behaves in much the same way. It is stronger in the foreground. The further away objects are, the bluer and grayer they become.

Left: *When color is used, the illusion of depth or distance is created by employing a paler tint of the color. However, when different colors are used each color must be assessed tonally and this can be a little more difficult as some colors are naturally stronger than others.*

Below left: *The same diagram, this time rendered in pencil. Practice with a variety of grades of pencil until you are able to apply a constant tone to the paper both on a small and a large area.*

Above: *Selecting the correct pencil and using the correct pressure on each area is the secret of a good tonal pencil drawing. The more you practice pencil technique the more variation you will obtain as your control of the medium improves.*

Above: *When pen and ink are used, pressure is of secondary importance. The density of the mark remains the same at all times. Tonal gradation is a question of the thickness of the line and the number of lines applied to the area.*

Above: *This is a good method of learning to use paint because the problems involved are reduced. The tonal value of different colors can be ignored while you concentrate on making the painting work using white and other color.*

Above: *When executing a full-color painting, you will need to understand how to mix different colors to the same tonal value so that you can make areas of the painting recede or come forward as required. Practice is the key to a successful technique.*

Light, atmosphere, and contrast

Light is the most influential element for a painter. Without it nothing exists visually, so we need to pay a great deal of attention to its behavior. It reveals not only the solidity of objects, but also the space they inhabit, and is instrumental in conveying atmosphere, mood, and the nature of color.

The result of light falling on an object is a cast shadow. You cannot have one without the other and the depth or darkness of the shadow is related to the intensity of light. It is important to ascertain the direction from which the light comes. In landscape painting it will depend on the position of the sun, which may be high or low, to the left, right, or behind you. It may be obscured by cloud. You must take notice of these variables before you begin. Study the differences between the effects that sunlight has on the planes as they recede from you, and what kinds of shadows are thrown.

If the light is strong, the shadows will be intense. If diffused by cloud, the shadows will be softer and less obvious.

Sunlight is not constant and its quality varies throughout the day. From dawn to dusk, each period of time has its own particular mood. Similarly, changes of weather and different cloud formations will give the light, and so the mood, a different aspect. These changes will often reveal space and distance more clearly, but being transitory may have to be overemphasized to do them justice.

Light in spring and summer will tend to be warmer in color and the shadows more crisply defined and full of contrast. In winter, the light is less intense, complicating the forms of the landscape. These different kinds of light will affect the mood and can also be exploited to create depth and a means of enhancing the composition.

Left: *The diagrams illustrate the importance of light and shadow. The top diagram appears flat and devoid of interest because the direction of the light source has been ignored. The lower two diagrams differ in both direction and color of cast shadow, suggesting different times of the day and their attendant moods.*

Above: Farms Near Auvers by Vincent van Gogh. The painting was executed in bright color with no reference to shadow. The result is a painting which exudes sunshine from its tapestry of brushmarks. Compare this with the painting by Norbert Goeneutte below, with its foreboding sky promising yet more snow. An unusual factor in this painting is the light color of the ground against which all other elements stand out in sharp contrast. Note also the comparative smoothness of the paint on the canvas.

Elements of landscape: buildings

The problem involved in rendering any element of a landscape is primarily one of visualization. This means deciding exactly what you see and, subsequently, deciding how to go about painting or drawing it. Probably the most formidable task facing the newcomer to painting is the decision about what is "seen". This is because everybody knows what houses, trees, and grass look like and this knowledge impairs observation.

Our understanding of the world is built upon experience, and this means that we recognize objects by their similarity to an idea of that object carried in the mind: we have a concept of the world against which to match objects. Once this match has been made, the object has been defined and it becomes ignored for the purposes of our normal day-to-day lives. This allows our conscious mind to concentrate on the job in hand while the subconscious takes care of perception.

Learning to see

The problem facing the newcomer is formidable because, in order to be able to paint, the tendency to ignore, and the preconcieved ideas allied to it, must be overcome. The people who say that they cannot paint are really saying that they cannot see and analyze their

Above and right: *The subjects on this page are treated from three different distances. Compare the amount of detail in each rendering; it is what is seen that should be included in a painting not what is known to be there. Once you have mastered your materials, observation is the key to successful work.*

vision in sufficient depth to be able to put it down on paper.

The illustrations on this and the following pages will attempt to provide some indication of the way in which a subject might be rendered, and the method of approaching the task. The activity is entirely personal, and the aim should be to find a method of working which is easiest for you. This will not be as difficult as it sounds because in art, as in all things, one person will find one method easier while another will assume a different approach which he will tend to use and develop because, for him, it is the easiest and most efficient.

Method and style

Do not be discouraged if you find that you cannot work in a particular way, or are unable to obtain a degree of finish as polished as some originals. A great part of what is known as an artist's style is simply the result of that person finding a method of working which is his own, and therefore easy for him to use, and developing it by constant practice with all kinds of materials.

There can be no hard and fast rules laid down about the way you learn to draw and paint. It will always be dependant on the stage you have reached in your development. In the early days, if you find one material easier to use, then by all means use it to the exclusion of all others until you have built up your confidence. You will often find that, later, other materials can be employed using a modified technique derived from your normal method of working.

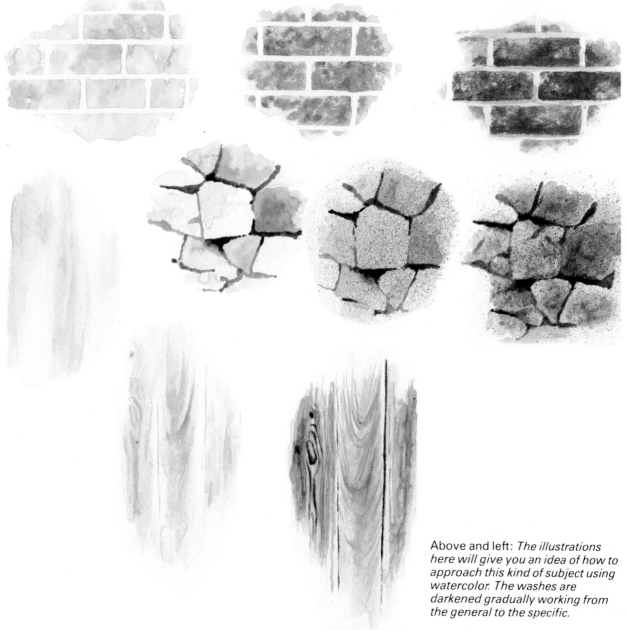

Above and left: *The illustrations here will give you an idea of how to approach this kind of subject using watercolor. The washes are darkened gradually working from the general to the specific.*

Elements of landscape: trees

It is the elements which you include or leave out of your drawings and paintings which make the finished work look convincing. To show the character of a tree or shrub you have to know something about its structure.

Like the human body with its bones and muscles, a tree or shrub has its trunk and branches. With the human body, however, the internal structure is permanently hidden and only seen on the dissecting table. Trees and shrubs, on the other hand, if they are deciduous, shed their covering of leaves annually.

To understand the structure of a tree or shrub means that you must study it in its dressed and undressed states; both have their part to play in describing the form. In winter, trees without leaves have just as much dignity and beauty as when fully laden.

Structure

A tree or shrub is made up of many small shapes. Apart from the main trunk, the branches, twigs, and shoots are a mass of elongated forms. The leaves which clothe the tree are further

Above and left: *Analyze the form and structure of trees in your landscape first. If the early definition is lightly drawn subsequent drawing or painting can be carried out without the need to erase the initial statement.*

Above: *Notice the difference in the treatment of foliage when it is further away. Attempting to paint every leaf individually would have resulted in a lifeless and unnatural appearance.*

numerous small shapes. If you attempt to draw a tree or shrub by concentrating on these small shapes the result will look unconvincing.

You should aim to work broadly and construct the overall shape of the tree, breaking the larger shapes into smaller ones as you proceed in order to avoid making a tight and labored image. Always work from the general toward the specific.

The character of trees and shrubs changes when seen in groups. Singly they may look static, but in a mass they take on rhythms and movements created by variations of color and shape. The color of trees and shrubs when contrasted with each other may also appear quite different than when seen singly.

Because of their structure, trees also possess a textural quality and pattern, which may change under certain circumstances; in the wind, in a raking, strong side light, or when contrasted with smooth, even backgrounds each tree will project a different character.

This textural quality or pattern will vary appreciably with the type of leaf. Some are thick and luscious, others thin and wispy; while painting, grasp it early, and depict it loosely and with feeling for the form.

It is worth keeping a sketchbook in which to practice drawing, and painting trees, both in detail and from a distance.

Above and left: *A step-by-step illustration of the method of painting a tree at a distance and the treatment of a tree trunk when seen at close quarters.*

Elements of landscape: skies and clouds

The sky is vastly important in landscape painting. Its tone, color, and light affects every part of the terrain. It can take up two-thirds of a canvas and be the prime subject or be reduced to a tiny strip at the top. Even so, the ground will reflect the character of the sky.

Skies vary with time of day. They may be intense in color or subtly tinted, depending on whether it is dawn, dusk, or midday. They may be clear or cloudy. If related to a strongly toned foreground, the sky will appear pale, conversely, if there is a great deal of sunlight on the ground, the sky will be rich and dense in color.

The appearance of a sky is rarely static. It is the inconstancy of sky and the light which comes from it which causes the rapid and radical change in the appearance of all the other elements in a landscape.

A sky is not like a curtain with the same hue from top to bottom. The gradations that take place are from dark above to lighter toward the horizon. If the sky is a rich blue overhead, it will become a lighter blue as it meets the horizon. The changes of color need not necessarily be of the same hue. Blue may turn to green or purple, and at dusk or dawn the sky may be shot with red, orange, and yellow. The colors may move through the whole spectrum; that is the source of its fascination. Learn to detect these changes, and use your brush either vigorously or smoothly to express the variations of depth and tone to enhance the particular qualities of skies at different times.

Nothing can change a sky more swiftly than clouds, which may either be blown across or appear to form before your very eyes.

Above left: *The technique used will vary with different skies. Here, watercolor was laid onto damp paper to create an effect of sunlight breaking through clouds after rain.*

Above right: *The contrast of an evening sky is best rendered by allowing each wash to dry to create a hard edge to the clouds.*

Right: *A combination of both techniques will often be necessary.*

Cloud formations alter so considerably, and so quickly that only by constant observation can you learn to record their individual characteristics. As Constable did, keep a record of them in a notebook devoted solely to the way clouds behave. It will be useful for the production of compositions later, as well as improving your knowledge of the types of cloud and ways of painting them.

Bear in mind that, although clouds are basically gaseous and weightless, they do reflect light, and often appear quite shapely and solid. Like solid forms, they possess clearly defined light and dark areas.

Clouds are literally suspended in space. To give the impression of depth, treat them as you would objects on the ground by the use of perspective and scale.

Cloud formations affect the landscape by creating rhythms and movements which echo or contrast with the forms beneath.

Top: *Two stages in the production of a skyscape using the alla prima method of oil painting. The first colors should be thinly applied to facilitate the laying in of the whites without destroying the colors.*

Above and below: *Three stages in the production of a sky using the traditional method of oil painting. Paint thinned with oil (known as a glaze) is painted over previously applied areas to intensify the effect.*

Elements of landscape: water

The qualities and character of large expanses of water such as seas, rivers, and lakes are quite different to small confined areas of water as in ponds, streams, and puddles. Most of the differences are due to the way light falls on the surface of the water because of the existence or lack of surrounding forms and how much movement there is.

The ripple of water is generally caused by wind or current. Sometimes, however, it is caused by birds, fish, boats, and people. Whatever the cause, water will reflect what is around and above it. The larger the area of water, the more of the sky it will reflect. Small areas of contained water are more likely to be still, and so will reflect with the clarity of a mirror.

Areas of water rarely look the same because winds and currents are not constant. The flowing stream one day may look like plate glass the next; you can never be sure how the surface will appear. The sky will also play its part and affect the reflection, so study all of them, static as well as fast-moving water, ripples as well as waves.

The following points should be borne in mind: though water always reflects what is around and above, the color reflected is always lower in tone than the original. Movement will fragment the reflection, slight movements interrupting the reflection without making it unrecognizable, strong movement completely obliterating it.

Left: *The changeable nature of water is reflected in these sketchbook extracts. The character changes according to the elements acting upon it and this is probably the fascination of water.*

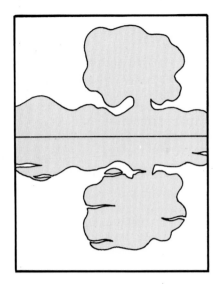
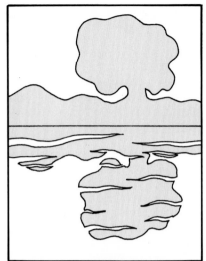

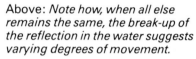

Above: *Note how, when all else remains the same, the break-up of the reflection in the water suggests varying degrees of movement.*

Left: *Refraction causes a great deal of difference also. Compare these two views of the same object. Note how the color value of the subject has changed.*

Below: *Monet began making studies of this lily pond during his mature period. The constantly changing character of its surface and depths held an allure which captivated him for the rest of his life.*

Methods of drawing: observation

When beginning to draw, experimentation with different materials is important, as is analysis of the structures of trees, rocks, and clouds. Draw freely and often and do not be put off by apparent failure. Keep all your drawings, even the bad ones. You may be surprised later looking back at them and they can provide a record of how much you have improved as you practice.

Making a start

To be confronted with a blank sheet of paper, a pencil, and a magnificent panorama can be as daunting for the experienced as for the beginner. How do you start? At what point can you decide that you have captured the essence of the scene?

The first thing to remember is not to try too hard. When you first look at a landscape, your immediate reaction will be complex. It will be difficult to unravel your feelings right away so do not try. Sit down and have a good long stare letting your eyes rove over the scene to let the overall image soak in. Do not make any effort to analyze what

you see, but accept it uncritically. Absorb it like a sponge. Make a few, simple, lightly drawn marks on your paper, indicating those aspects of the landscape which you find important. Making heavy, dark marks on white paper too soon only adds to the difficulties you are trying to resolve. Draw with light, broken lines or dots to get the "feel" of the pencil on the paper.

These marks are only exploratory and there is no need to erase them should they appear to be in the wrong place. Leave them as a guide, against which to gauge corrections.

Add a few scribbles of tone. Scribbled or smudged tones, drawn gently, will also help you get the "feel" of the pencil on the paper. The tones will advance the drawing and make the image more convincing.

To bring what you are drawing into sharper focus, look more at the scene in front of you and less at your drawing. Paradoxically, looking more at your drawing and less at the scene is likely to confuse the image rather than clarify it. Concentrating on the scene allows your hand to respond instinctively and so carry out its job more naturally.

Trust the process of looking and letting the pencil make marks without effort, and curb your desire to criticize and interfere with what emerges on the paper. By being too critical you destroy the natural flow, fail to enjoy what you are doing, and cause the drawing to become contrived.

Allow your drawing to become gradually darker and stronger in tone until all the paper is covered. This will give you confidence. By pushing your drawings too far initially, you will learn how far you need to go.

Drawing outdoors using this method can be done in a sketchbook or on paper clipped to a light drawing board and held on your knee. An easel is not as necessary as it would be for oil painting but do hold your board or sketchbook upright from time to time to compare what you are doing with what you are looking at. Stand away from your drawing, and view it from a distance by placing it upright against a wall or stone, or even on the ground. "Distancing" yourself from your work allows you to respond to it more objectively.

Left: *During the early stages of a drawing, it can be helpful to use a pencil held at arm's length to measure the relative proportions of elements in the landscape. However, use it only as an initial guide or your drawing may become cramped and stiff.*

Above right: *The first lines of a drawing lightly laid in.*

Center right: *Reinforcement of the initial statement with some tone added.*

Below right: *The completed drawing. Note the slight emphasis placed upon the pier; compare this with the photograph of the scene on the opposite page.*

Methods of drawing: selection

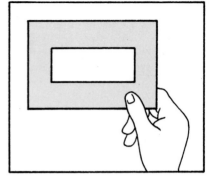

The first step in drawing landscapes is to spend time looking before making exploratory marks in line and tone. The second step is to be more selective in what you choose and the way it is interpreted through emphasis.

Emphasizing the important aspects of what you see will make your work more effective, and so more pleasing to look at. But they must be aspects which you find important; do not be led, for subconsciously you know what is important to you.

As has been pointed out, nature is not confined to a rectangle. Neither are your eyes restricted to the accepted range of 60 degrees. By moving your head or letting your eyes rove over a scene, you can take in 180 degrees at a glance without moving your body.

You can either try to draw the whole panorama or select a particular area that appeals to you, not only across the landscape, but into it as well.

If you use your eyes like the lens of a camera that can zoom in on a part and enlarge it, to the exclusion of what borders it, you will find that you can filter out what you do not need of a distant scene and enlarge the section you want. If it is too close, then you can reduce it.

To show how this works, try looking at a scene through a rectangle cut out of a piece of card, preferably black. By holding the card nearer or further away from you, you can completely alter the view you are looking at. If you move the card across the scene you will be amazed how different the views are when isolated in this way by the card viewfinder. As you gain experience, you will find you can dispense with the viewfinder.

Emphasis

When you select a part from the whole, your choice places an emphasis on that part as being special. It is quite possible to select a number of parts for emphasis yet find the view as a whole uninteresting or unmanageable. On the other hand, you might find that the whole view and its parts deserve attention.

Opposite: *A viewfinder can be cut from a piece of card.*

Right and below: *Two drawings produced from the viewpoint shown opposite. Almost anything can provide a subject for a good drawing: that is the fascination of landscape work.*

Methods of oil painting: alla prima

There are as many ways to paint in oils as there are painters, each has his own method of expression. But fundamental to any personally evolved method are two basic styles which underlie all others: the direct method or Alla Prima, and the Traditional method.

Completing a painting in one session in full color, with opaque paint so that any previous drawing or underpainting tends to be obliterated and has little or no modifying effect on the subsequent layers, is referred to as "Alla Prima." It was first used in the nineteenth century when many painters began painting landscapes directly in the open air.

It is a method that landscape painters still favor today because it is an ideal way of completing a painting when there are problems with the weather or available time. It may also better suit your temperament.

Affinities with the Traditional method do exist so that you do not need to turn somersaults to accommodate both styles. Learning about one will help the other. For example, you can draw in your composition as you would with the Traditional method, or make preparatory studies or sketches beforehand. It is, however, essentially painting in one go and preparation is not necessary except for the underpainting or priming coat of paint.

Tonal priming

The essential point about oil painting is that, since it is an opaque or obliterating medium, you can organize your tones more convincingly if you start from the middle to dark end of the tonal scale rather than from the lightest: the white canvas.

Very simply this means that, unlike watercolor where you work from light to dark for the best results, with oil you work more from dark to light. However, for practical purposes it is best to start with the mid range of tones so that you can gauge more accurately the intensity of the lights and darks.

To facilitate this part of the process, ensure that your surfaces have a light to medium tone on them before you begin. Prior to going out, prepare a thin

Left: *The scene from which the painting on these pages was produced. Note how closely the colors of the original subject have been followed.*

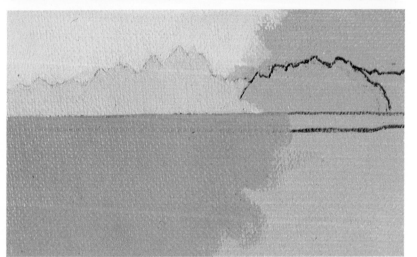

Left: *The initial stages of the painting. The left-hand side of the painting has the first flat colors laid in while the right-hand side shows the tonal priming of the canvas and the basic drawing.*

creamy mixture of a quick-drying foundation white (some artist's colormen make a specially prepared white for this purpose). This is tinted with a little raw umber and your support is covered completely with it. It does not matter if the result is streaky as this will help animate your painting. Do make sure that there are no ridges of thick paint in evidence as this will interfere with your one-coat Alla Prima effect.

Drying mediums

The problem with Alla Prima painting is that, if your paint is too wet, the effects you require may not be easy to produce. Additionally, if your painting is wet, when completed these effects may be spoiled. It is worth experimenting with a drying medium which will resolve the problem without interfering with the way you paint.

Above right: *The foreground, background, and sky have been worked up to their correct tonal balance.*

Center right: *The line of the trees has been broadly applied; the paler trees will be painted over and into these to push them back.*

Below right: *The completed painting. The foreground is laid in with just enough detail to prevent it detracting from the center of interest – the trees and mountain range behind. In a composition of this nature it is the abstract quality of the bands of color and texture which are important.*

There are many kinds available but the most successful is the newest type made with an alkyd resin which is safe and easy to use. It will not damage the painted surface by cracking as it dries and is pleasant to paint with. You can use it in your dipper, either neat or diluted with turpentine, depending on how quickly you want the paint to dry. There are also two thicker versions which will help to create an effective impasto.

Methods of oil painting: traditional

The Traditional method of painting is slower than Alla Prima because there are more stages involved in the process. It is the ideal method if you want a more considered approach which will produce a greater degree of finish in the completed work.

The Traditional method can be used outdoors or in the studio. Working inside will be considered in the next section but, whichever you do, an easel is an essential piece of equipment. It will allow you the freedom to concentrate on mixing colors properly and to see clearly what you are doing and how you are progressing. By standing back from the easel, you can relate more easily what you are looking at in the landscape with how you are painting it. Moreover, it is easier to paint on a vertical support and it cuts out unwanted reflected light that might make the painted surface shine unpleasantly while you are working.

To begin, define precisely the part of the landscape you are going to paint as you may have to work from it for more than one session. Make a number of preliminary studies of your subject first, in the manner suggested in the section on drawing.

Prepare your surfaces before going out, with a mid-toned tint of raw umber and white.

When you are satisfied with your viewpoint, draw the basic composition on the tinted surface with charcoal pencil or a brush and diluted raw umber paint. Keep it simple, almost diagrammatic, avoiding detail.

When the drawing is dry, commence painting over it with color. This too should be broad but near in color and tone to what you are looking at.

Above: *A painting completed using the Traditional method of oil painting. The main difference between Alla Prima and traditional methods of painting is the thickness of the paint used for the overpainting. When painting a subject in one go, the paint does not have sufficient time to dry. Therefore, to prevent unwanted mixing of the colors, the paint is applied more thickly. The traditional approach, on the other hand, allows* the paint a certain amount of drying time and subsequent coats are often applied more thinly so that the underpainting glows through creating greater depth and more subtle, jewel-like qualities. For example, when a green is required it is quite possible to underpaint using yellow and follow this with a thin glaze of blue. The result will glow with an inner life and intensity that is lacking in a single coat of opaque color. It remains possible, as with *the Alla Prima method of painting, to correct mistakes by scraping out and repainting the area with new color. The area cleaned should be reasonably dry before the new coat of paint is applied to the surface. When scraping paint from the canvas it can be difficult to remove every scrap of pigment because of the grain. Don't be over fussy about this, as long as they are dry, small remnants can be left to modify the surface adding texture and interest to the area.*

As you will be working on the painting for some time, spend plenty of time simply looking and mixing and proportionally less in painting. Painting too rapidly can lead to muddled and muddy colors in the end result.

The process can be summed up as: broad shapes first, moving gradually to smaller and more precise shapes. Detail last, freely executed brush strokes first, more carefully controlled brush marks last, thin paint first, fat or thick paint later.

Changing your mind as often as the situation demands is eminently possible with oils if you observe these conditions, and doing so is a necessary part of producing a good painting.

Right: *The painting in its first stage. The basic drawing has been done and the areas filled in with flat color.*

Right: *Some basic background detail has been added and the clouds have been blocked in.*

Right: *The clouds and mountains are more fully modelled and the painting requires only the foreground detail to complete it.*

Studies for an oil painting

Working in the studio, rather than outdoors, allows more freedom to use memory and imagination but, as the only reference to landscape will be through your notes and studies, it will involve a slightly different approach to be certain they are used to advantage.

Working indoors may be forced upon you by bad weather, or other circumstances beyond your control. To take some previously made drawings and watercolors and work them up into an oil painting is as good a way of expressing yourself as being in front of the real thing.

Above: *This study was produced from the scene shown in the photograph on the left. Remembering that you can never have too much information from which to work, as much detail as possible was worked into the drawing.*

Firstly, it will be appreciated that working on the spot will furnish valuable experience that will aid memory, but if you intend to rely on drawings and color sketches which are too brief or too few, they will fail either to jog the memory or stimulate the imagination. Therefore both experience and thorough studies should be your aim when working outside.

Drawings for this process should be concerned with detail as well as broad statements, light and atmosphere, changes of weather, formations of clouds, studies of trees, both in the form of drawings and colored and written notes.

As a result studies may only be fragments of information, but as long as they are carefully observed they will be of value.

Azure sky

Deep blue, green pine trees with reddish, brown trunk

Brilliant yellow foliage tinged with Alizarin Crimson and ochre with touches of sap green interlaced with dark brown branches

Olive green trees behind house

Very strong, dark shadows on trunks of trees

Buff or off white foliage.

Gray brown trunks of trees with intense shadows

Gray windows — note shadows and reflections in windows

Viridian and gray blue trees in background

Strong shadows on front of building

Viridian leaves on hedge — some orange leaves on top of hedge

Blue, gray road with payne's gray shadows — strong contrast

Above: *An alternative method of making color notes is to write them on a sheet of tracing paper fixed to the original study.*

Left: *Detail abstracted from the foreground of the scene for special attention. It is worth studying man-made structures in the landscape as these are the things that can be difficult to work from memory.*

Completing an oil painting

Completing an oil painting in the studio from sketches and studies relies, in the initial stages, on composition. It helps you select the best possible subject by choosing views that accord best with the format you are using and deploying the shapes and colors to the best possible effect by paying attention to the dynamics of the forms you are observing.

Composition is used in the studio in much the same way except that you have the flexibility to select and arrange the raw material — sketches and studies — in any way you wish. You are not restricted by what is in front of you as you would be outside. You can distribute the colors and forms in the way that you feel is appropriate. Your choices will still be limited by the shape and, possibly, the size of your support, and the way you assemble your material will have to take into consideration the basic principles discussed in the section on composition.

Having said this, you will discover as you work that you can make as many alternative arrangements as you like until you are satisfied everything is presented in the best possible way for the purpose intended.

Making a number of exploratory rough drawings from your initial sketches is a practical way of ensuring that the "happiest" solution is arrived at. You can then enlarge the best of them to the size you wish to use for the painting and transfer the drawing to your painting surface. You can begin drawing straight onto the support or scale it up first by squaring.

Once you have transferred your composition to the tinted surface, the procedure for carrying out the painting is much the same as suggested in the previous section. The only difference is that you must rely on memory and imagination to replace an actual landscape in front of you. Substitute your memory and imagination for the landscape and use your drawings and studies as props. The drawing need not be strictly adhered to should you find that your creative impulses are fighting to be unleashed.

Painting indoors away from any kind of landscape that you can refer to is perhaps the most enjoyable way to express yourself. On the other hand, it is more difficult for the inexperienced. If you persevere, however, and practice both kinds of approach, you will find that each will help the other to progress.

Right: *The process of squaring up a drawing is quite a simple one. The number of squares used is not important as long as there are enough to provide sufficient guidance. It should also be remembered, that the proportions of the two surfaces must be the same.*

Below: *The painting completed in the studio following the sequence of steps shown on the opposite page. The initial drawing was produced from the studies on the previous page with alteration made to improve the composition.*

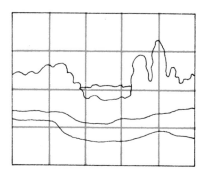

A canvas of similar proportion is selected to receive the enlarged drawing and both surfaces are squared as shown here.

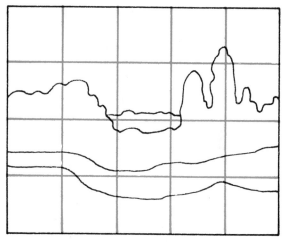

Methods of watercolor painting

A watercolor is produced with water-soluble paint, a brush, and white paper. Since the paint layers on the surface are very thin, light is reflected from the paper through the washes to produce the lightness and luminosity of color that characterizes this type of paint. This is the medium's prime attraction.

The luminosity of watercolor depends on preserving transparency at all costs. Should it be lost, the only resort is to remove some of the paint by running the painting under a fawcet and leaving it to dry or, failing that, to begin again. Should white paint be used to remedy this loss, the result, unless done with uncommon skill, will look inconsistent. If a painter prefers opacity, the addition of white to the colors at the outset will produce a desirable, but totally different, result to transparent watercolor. This kind of paint is commercially available as gouache.

To obtain the best results from watercolor requires practice in laying both flat and graduated washes. The paper must be allowed to play its part, and often, leaving an area of white paper showing through will do more for the intensity of color and the overall effect of the painting than anything else. Beyond this there is very little that can be said. Practice and experience are the keys to successful watercolor work.

The basic selection of twelve colours which follows will cater for just about every kind of landscape that you might encounter: lemon yellow, chrome yellow, vermillion, alizarin crimson, French ultramarine, Antwerp or Windsor blue, viridian, oxide of chromium, raw sienna, raw umber, light red, paynes gray.

Blacks can be made with raw umber and viridian.

Above left: *The basic watercolor wash. Practice until you can get this completely flat without stains and dark patches.*

Above right: *The gradated wash should also be practiced until the change from dark to light can be carried out smoothly.*

Left: *The overlapping of several washes should be practiced so that you become acquainted with the way in which colors are modified.*

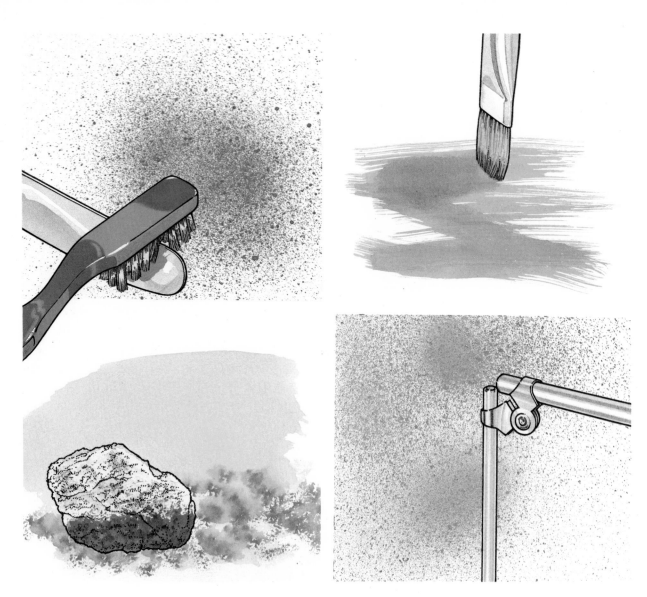

Traditional watercolor technique is described on the next page; there are, however, several methods which can be employed to heighten the effect with the aid of easily, and cheaply, obtainable tools.

As an alternative to laying washes with a brush, a small, natural sponge may be used. On a large area, this has the advantage of enabling paint to be applied faster and is therefore likely to produce a more even coverage as the wet areas run together and the pigment spreads more efficiently. The sponge may also be used to remove areas of paint to create highlights and, when used with a slightly thicker wash, the paint can be applied with a dabbing motion to produce a textured effect.

The hog hair brush is basically an oil painting tool which, when used with watercolor paint, can produce a textured brush mark and provide direction within a wash which would otherwise be flat. Practice is required to get the desired effect; a wet brush will produce a soft mark while a dryer brush will produce hard, outstanding lines.

The use of a spray diffuser can create some interesting results by producing spots of color on the paper. The color can be modified by over-spraying with a second color when the first is dry. Test the color on a spare piece of paper as you may wish to strengthen or dilute the pig-

ment. Always wait until the test-piece is dry before application to the painting as the paint will invariably dry to a paler tint. By cutting a mask from thin card or by using a commercial masking liquid, a hard-edged effect can be obtained.

A toothbrush can be used to good effect providing a "spatter" of paint similar to that provided by a spray-diffuser but with greater variation. Again, card or liquid masks may be used to create a hard edge.

Finally, try using a drinking straw to blow pools of pigment placed on the paper with a brush. A mesh of marks can be created in this way, and if the technique is used carefully some stunning effects can result.

Watercolor technique

Unless a very free treatment is required, a watercolor painting should proceed from a lightly drawn pencil sketch. This can be as detailed or as cursory as you wish, but remember that a more detailed sketch will produce a tighter end result.

The first wash

Begin at the top of the paper so that other washes can be laid down while the first is drying. The wash is applied with the largest brush suitable for the area to be covered and it should be well loaded with the wash color. These initial washes should be kept pale to allow for later adjustment and detail. Prop up the board so that gravity will draw the paint down the page: the angle of the slope defines the amount of control over the wash.

Draw the brush across the paper, starting at the top and maintaining a pool at the base of the brush stroke. Reload your brush and start again below the first strip of paint making sure that the brush stroke touches the pool above for the full width of the wash. If the brush does miss at any point, you will have to live with a small area of white paper showing. Do not scrub at the paper in an attempt to get the wash even, it will never work. The effect can in fact add to the quality of the painting. Carry on in this way until the lowest extremity of the wash is reached. The brush can now be dried and used to mop away the pool of paint which has descended to the bottom of the colored area.

Other considerations

This is the basic technique and requires only minor modification to cater for all applications. The first wash applied will probably be the sky and, if there are any clouds to be included, these areas must be avoided so that they will sparkle with diffused

light when the work is completed. The same will be true of any pale details surrounded by dark areas lower in the painting.

While the first wash is drying the second wash can be applied, but make sure that the area to be covered does not touch the wet area already laid down otherwise the two washes will run together. If you are in any doubt about your ability to control these washes, wait until the paper is dry before proceeding.

If a rough or toothed paper is used and you wish to have a "spatter" of white paper showing through the whole wash, less water is used: this is known as "dry brush" technique and can produce a very lively result. It will take time and practice to master the materials but the rewards will be worth the effort.

Above: *When you are out on a painting expedition, keep your eyes open for interesting aspects close to you. It is far too easy to look right past a view which would make a perfectly good painting when seeking a suitable composition.*

Above right: *It is the abstract qualities of the composition which make this subject worth painting and this is already evident in the drawing.*

Above far right: *The drawing after application of the first washes.*

Above: *The woodpile has been worked up and the first of many washes applied to the leaves in the foreground. The wood panelling of the shack has been laid in using a dry brush technique to suggest the grain of the wood.*

Above: *The completed painting is close in appearance to the original subject. The limited depth of field heightens the abstract quality of the painting which relies upon harmonious color, pattern and texture for its effect.*

Foregrounds

Foregrounds play such an important role in landscape painting that they are well worth studying separately. Landscape painters, both past and present, have relied a great deal on what could be done with a foreground and their work will repay study.

When looking at a landscape that you may want to paint, it is quite easy to overlook the foreground. The tendency is to look for the middle and background, quite forgetting that the scene before you starts at your feet.

The great landscape painters were always careful to examine the foreground in case they missed something valuable.

Many painters, for instance, pay so much attention to the foreground that it takes up most of the painting and becomes the subject and focal point. Derelict barns, walls, fences, hedges, pools, ponds, gates, farm machinery, fallen trees, waterfalls, in short, anything that takes your eye can serve as a subject, or a good foreground.

Generally, foregrounds are included to give the landscape more life, or more authenticity. A foreground well-established in the composition will give balance to whatever else is included. It can also help to suggest space. It can lead the eye into the picture to where you want your visual emphasis. It can be used to fill parts of the painting that would otherwise be devoid of interest.

There is no end to the versatility of the foreground, provided that you pay attention to it when you are out sketching. Once you are familiar with the visual characteristics: large, clear, strongly colored, the foreground will assert itself more firmly in your paintings.

Make a point from time to time of studying foregrounds only. Fill a notebook with different kinds. You will never regret doing so as these drawings will always be useful when you are working in the studio. If it does nothing else, the experience will make you more conscious of their contribution and will increase your observational skills.

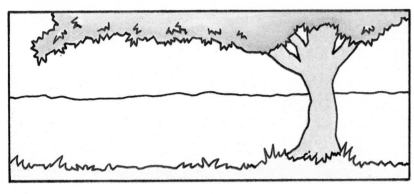

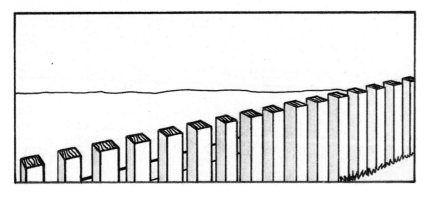

Top left: The tree and grass in the foreground is used as a device to frame the middle and background.

Center left: In this illustration the foreground motif is the focal point and is supported by the background.

Below left: The foreground again used as a device, this time to lead the eye across and into the picture.

Opposite top: Detail from Long Grass with Butterflies by van Gogh, a superb painting in which the foreground is the subject relying upon color and the brush mark to provide interest.

Opposite bottom: In this detail from Monet's painting, Bathers at la Grenouillere, the boats in the foreground lead the eye to the focal point of the painting – the bathers silhouetted against the light entering under the trees.

About other media

Watercolor and oil are the two traditional and most widely used media employed by artists.

Apart from oil and watercolor, other paints in common use today are gouache, acrylic, and alkyd.

Gouache

When white paint is added to watercolor to give opacity and covering power, it is known as gouache. It is specially mixed and is available in tubes and jars for easy application.

Gouache has a quality and feel somewhere between watercolor and tempera and can also be used like oils, though this is not recommended as the glue binders are not powerful enough to hold the pigment together.

Gouache is a splendid medium for those who wish to take a painting further than watercolor allows. Unlike tempera, which dries bone hard, gouache can be easily reactivated with water.

This means that when over-painting there is a danger of picking up the coat beneath and spoiling your colors.

For a harder drying paint that has affinities with most other paints, the recently developed acrylics have many qualities that are well worth exploiting.

Acrylic

Traditional paints are made with dry pigments bound with natural glues to hold them together and make them workable. These "binders" determine the characteristics of the paint, whether they are thin or thick, slow or quick drying. Binders that can be diluted with water include gums, egg yolk, and milk, and these dry very quickly. Oil paint, on the other hand, is bound with linseed, poppy, or nut oil, is diluted with turpentine or mineral spirits and takes much longer to dry.

Acrylic is unique insofar as it has a man-made binder which consists of acrylic resin. It is in fact a plexiglass-like plastic, and is very durable and does not darken when dry. Acrylic can be diluted with water and can be used in much the same way as gouache and watercolor. But, because of the nature of the binder, it can also be used straight from the tube, employing a technique similar to oil painting.

Acrylic dries very hard and cannot be reactivated with water. It can therefore be over-painted without fear of picking up the paint underneath. This means that palette and brushes need to be kept scrupulously clean because, once dry, the paint is very hard to remove.

The colors are bright and

Below: *The proximity of this subject allows the use of a "posterized" technique. The opacity and flatness of gouache makes it the ideal medium for dealing with this kind of motif.*

easily mixed. They lack the range found in oil paints, but there are enough, at least fifty, to fill most requirements.

You can apply acrylic paint to paper, board, and canvas, with or without priming it first.

Acrylic is a safe and versatile paint which, because of its quick-drying properties, has many advantages over oil. If you are unused to a quick-drying paint, especially when used thickly, it is advisable to work indoors before taking them outside where they dry even quicker.

As with all other media, practice is the key to producing good work.

Alkyd

Alkyd is the newest paint on the market. Because of its binder, alkyd resin, it dries faster and harder. Alkyd is similar to oil but, because of its fast-drying properties, it facilitates the use of traditional oil painting techniques such as scumbling, impasto, and glazing.

Alkyds dry to an even sheen, unlike oil, thus obviating the need to restore dull patches with a retouching varnish.

The pigments used in alkyd are exactly the same as in oil, but because of the alkyd resin binder there is less yellowing the paint film is more durable and less liable to damage.

Alkyds are stiffer to handle than oils, and need more patience in mixing. The addition of a little mineral spirits should be sufficient to bring the paint to a working consistency.

Because Alkyds dry comparatively quickly it is more economical to put out less paint than you would normally do when using oils.

Again, before trying outdoors, you should experiment inside until you get the feel of the paint and become familiar with the unique drying properties. The equipment you need is exactly the same as with oil. They are perfectly compatible with oils, though if they are mixed together the drying characteristic will be altered.

Above: *Acrylics allow the use of glazes while speed of working is maintained. Great subtlety is therefore possible with the medium even when the painting is completed in one sitting.*

Analysis

Much can be learned from the great painters of the past and one of the best ways of learning from them is to analyze their painting.

An effective way to analyze a painting to discover the important lines, proportions, balances, and rhythms is to get a good reproduction – a postcard will do – of your favorite work and to trace the basic keyshapes and lines as shown here. Use a transparent tracing paper or thin layout paper so that you can see the reproduction clearly.

You can then transfer the tracing onto a piece of paper or card and broadly paint in the colors, to see how it is related to the composition as a whole and to see how it functions.

You may, as many great artists in the past did, do a free translation of a painting in your own style using the original as a basis from which to work. You may add your own location, time of day, and any important details required.

You can also copy the original, as this can equally well give you an insight into how a painting was arrived at. To get the maximum value, it is important to paint your copy directly from the original painting and not from a reproduction. It is usually possible to arrange this with an art gallery if sufficient notice is given.

Working from a reproduction is only useful for general analysis or as a starting point for a painting of your own.

As well as analyzing the works of the great artists it is vitally important that you also enjoy simply looking at them. Do not approach the gallery on every visit with the intention of working at analysis. Give yourself the opportunity sometimes to do nothing but bathe in the beauty of the work.

Opposite: Water-lily Pond *by Monet. A subtly composed piece of work with the bridge as focal point. It is the tonal values of the lilies and reflections in the water, and the vegetation surrounding the pond which creates movement and interest in the painting. The bridge frames the pond and its curve sets up a motion which carries the eye round the painting.*

Right: *The abstract quality of Monet's* Poplars on the Epte *is evident in the swirling rhythm of the trees and the nature of the brush marks.*

Below left: *This keyline diagram illustrates the main direction lines of Monet's painting.*

Below right: *The addition of the main areas of color illustrates just how abstract Monet's vision of this scene was.*

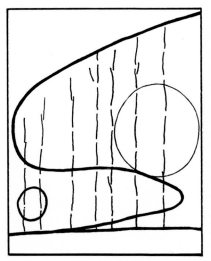

Appreciation

Landscape painting flourished significantly in England in the latter part of the eighteenth century, and reached an influential peak with Constable and Turner, which makes it very difficult to compile any appreciation of landscape painting without mentioning the debt that is owed to them.

Nor can we ignore that they too were influenced and encouraged in turn by painters like Claude, Poussin, and Jacob van Ruisdael. It is this constant passing on of knowledge from generation to generation that has enriched the art of painting through the ages.

Looking at paintings by either accepted masters or lesser lights will enrich your understanding and enjoyment of painting landscape. We have nature on the one hand and a surface on the other: the problem is to translate one into the other. By studying how other painters achieved it, you will benefit from their experience and increase your own painting skills.

Though, when looking at styles of painting they may look widely different, the problems of picture making — getting nature onto the canvas — remain the same for us all.

Top: Salisbury Cathedral from the Meadow *by the English artist John Constable.*

Bottom: The Avenue, Middelharnis *by Meyndert Hobbema.*